Money Magic
with Annuities

Great Ideas
for
Creative Investors

by
Richard W. Duff, J.D., CLU

RWD Enterprises
Denver

Published by RWD Enterprises,
1777 So. Harrison St. #625
Denver, CO 80210 U.S.A.

tel 303-756-3599
fax 303-691-0474
RWDuffCLU@aol.com
www.mcomm.com/duff/

*Book and cover design by Robert Marcus Graphics,
Sebastopol, California.
Cartoons by L. Pesson, Denver, Colorado.
Printed in the United States of America.
First Edition, 2000.*

ISBN 1-882703-01-4

Introduction

Annuities are almost magical in the world of financial planning. Where else can you find a tax-deferred insured investment that promises the return of your money and interest on it as well? Who wouldn't want something that:

¤ Pays a guaranteed current rate of interest (perhaps 6 percent-1999) where the principal is also guaranteed—a *fixed* annuity, or

¤ Provides a guaranteed minimum rate of interest (perhaps 3 percent)—where the principal is also guaranteed, and stock market-like returns are credited only on the *upside*—an e*quity indexed* annuity.

¤ Protects Social Security payments from federal income taxes.

¤ May provide income that doesn't disqualify a family member for Medicaid benefits.

Both fixed and equity-indexed annuities are strictly regulated in all 50 states, and are backed by State Guaranty Insurance Funds that usually shelter up to $100,000 if the insurer ever gets into financial trouble. Plain and simple, these annuities are safe, secure and as attractive financially as any investment you can possible think of. All interest is tax-deferred under the law. In many states, the annuity account is also protected from your creditors.

If you prefer equities, moreover, look to the *variable* annuity. These are annuity policies that invest in almost any mutual fund in the marketplace. With these, you give-up the minimum guarantees and State Guaranty Insurance, but you'll still have tax deferral and any creditor protection provided by the law.

Money Magic With Annuities explains how annuities solve real financial problems—your problems. This is not a basic primer, but a guide to mastering the subtleties and investment characteristics of this special investment tool—so that you can achieve your personal objectives.

Here's my recommendation: Read *Money Magic* carefully, and make a list of comments and questions as you read. Then, share these with your financial adviser. You might even ask him or her to diagram how these ideas apply to your situation. If you are really serious about building your wealth, learn how creative investors use annuities to improve their financial circumstances so you can do the same.

If you want to study up on the subject, here are some excellent books I recommend:

(1) Gordon K. Williamson, *Getting Started In Annuities,* John Wiley & Sons (1999). This is must reading. It isn't difficult, and it gives the basics about all types of annuities, and then some.

(2) Bruce F. Wells, *All About Variable Annuities From The Inside Out,* Irwin Professional Publishing

(1995). This book answers questions on annuities that invest in equities. I place it at an intermediate level.

(3) Darlene K. Chandler, JD, CLU, ChFC, *The Annuity Handbook, A Guide to Nonqualified Annuities*, The National Underwriter Company (1994). This paperback is more technical, but if your funds are heavily invested in annuities, you'll find this information helpful through the years.

It is only possible to measure the value of annuities by estimating future interest rates and returns in the equities market place. In *Money Magic*, I make the following assumptions, unless otherwise noted:

¤ Fixed annuities earn a constant 6 percent tax deferred rate of interest.

¤ Variable annuities earn a constant 12 percent tax deferred rate of interest.

¤ Your annuity program is equally blended between fixed and variable policies, and it earns a constant 9 percent tax deferred rate of interest.

¤ A blended investment portfolio earns 9 percent rate of return—6 percent after current taxes.

¤ Your personal income tax (federal and state) bracket is 33 percent.

¤ Your personal estate tax bracket is 50 percent.

Also, here's a refresher on a few financial concepts and annuity definitions employed by *Money Magic:*

¤ *Present Value* is a current sum which grows to another sum *(future value)* after a period of time, given a constant rate of return. Or, it is a current sum which pays out a set annual amount over a period of time, given a constant rate of return.

¤ *The Rule of 72* is a shortcut to determine how long it takes for capital to double and double again. For example, if you invest $100,000 and earn 9 percent per annum, you can divide 72 by 9 and learn that your money (ii) doubles to $200,000 in about 8 years. In this example, your money is worth $400,000 (2 doubles) after 16 years if the investment continues to earn 9 percent. It is worth $3.2 million (5 doubles) after 40 years.

To apply this concept in another way, let's assume someone acquired a farm in 1940 for $10,000, and today (2000), it's worth $320,000. You wonder what is the average rate of return. Use the Rule of 72 to determine this. Count the amount of "doubles"— 1940 to 2000 on your fingers—$10,000 to $20,000; $20,000 to $40,000; $40,000 to $80,000; $80,000 to $160,000; and $160,000 to $320,000—the answer is five. Now, divide 60 years (2000 less 1940) by five— the answer is 12. Finally, divide 72 by 12—the answer is 6. Therefore, the farm has appreciated at a 6 percent average annual rate of return over this 40 year period.

¤ *Single Premium Deferred or Immediate Annuities:* Where an insurer permits only one deposit into the policy. *Flexible premium deferred annuity policies* permit regular and ongoing deposits.

¤ *Commercial Annuities:* These are contracts with an insurance company where money is deposited to earn a given rate of return.

¤ *Deferred Annuities:* Where funds invested in an annuity accumulate savings over the years—sometimes called Accumulation Annuities.

¤ *Immediate Annuities:* When a deferred annuity (or a single premium immediate annuity) policy pays out income on a monthly, quarterly, semi-annual or annual basis—sometimes called Payout Annuities. These contracts usually make payments for one lifetime—a *life annuity;* sometimes they pay for two lifetimes—a *joint and survivor annuity.* When they guarantee payments for a set period, e.g., 10 years, this is called a *term certain annuity.* They can also pay for life with a minimum term, a *life annuity with a term certain.*

¤ *Annuitant:* This is the person whose life expectancy measures the amount you receive from an immediate annuity (or a deferred annuity when it is eventually annuitized).

¤ *Policyowner:* This is the party who has all rights and privileges under the annuity policy. For example, the policyowner can change a beneficiary, withdraw sums from a deferred annuity, pledge a policy, and determine who receives income when a deferred annuity policy is annuitized (and becomes an immediate annuity).

Here is a brief background on each of the 20 Great Ideas:

Great Idea #1 describes how to structure gifts of annuities for young children for their eventual retirement. And it compares an annuity with taxable investments earning 9 percent (6 percent after federal taxes @ your 33 percent income tax rate). This is the first Great Idea to assume a 9 percent blended annual rate of return on annuities. It also begins a discussion of the Rule of 72 concept and the doubling of money over many years.

Great Idea #2 advocates the use of annuities to transfer wealth for generations to come, using grandchild's vested trusts. It also compares annuities with investments that you acquire personally.

Great Idea #3 explains how annuities can build an education fund, using the Uniform Gift to Minors Act. It compares them to other investments where income is taxed to parents under the so-called "Kiddie Tax" rules.

Great Idea #4 shows how annuities compare to an Individual Retirement Account (IRA). An analysis shows that it may even be better to invest (outside an IRA) in annuities than to invest in the IRA itself.

Great Idea #5 introduces the concept of a private annuity—the sale of property to a family member in exchange for a lifetime income. It also describes the facts and circumstances where this strategy has special appeal.

Great Idea #6 shows how to sidestep a penalty tax when taking distributions from an annuity policy. In understandable terms, it compares pre-59-$\frac{1}{2}$ installment payments with an immediate annuity making lifetime payments. It also introduces the concept of present value.

Great Idea #7 explains how annuities are used to take distributions from an IRA beginning at or after your age 59-$\frac{1}{2}$. Compared with so-called "minimum distributions," annuities will simplify your tax planning.

Great Idea #8 combines IRA annuities and payments on a home mortgage. This is one way to "convert" an IRA into cash in your pocket. If you have a large IRA and a nearly debt-free home, you'll find this idea almost magical.

Great Idea #9 employs an annuity to pay fixed living expenses—a convenient method of handling your cash flow. If you don't like to spend countless hours "in front of your checkbook," you'll really like this simple strategy.

Great Idea #10 shows how annuities improve your financial station in life. It compares life and term certain annuities with other liquid investments, including a Treasury 30 year long-bond.

Great Idea #11 compares annuities (and life insurance) to CDs, Treasuries and bonds. The assumption is that a mix of Certificates of Deposits, Treasury investments and corporate bonds averaging a 6 percent annual rate of interest do not perform as well as annuities and insurance combined in a creative way. This is one of the best ways to increase retirement income, and pass more wealth to family at the same time. It deserves serious attention.

Great Idea #12 combines life insurance with annuities in an irrevocable trust—funding a life insurance policy with an immediate annuity. It compares this strategy with a Crummey Trust where you make annual gifts that beneficiaries can withdraw.

Great Idea #13 splits an annuity premium between two policies—split annuities. The financial results are interesting because this strategy actually beats a single annuity in most cases.

Great Idea #14 explains how to replace one annuity policy with another contract—a 1035 exchange. This is one of the few exchanges of property that can be tax-free under the Internal Revenue Code. But, you must do it with care. Many advisers aren't fully aware of how to complete this transaction correctly, and this Idea explains the "ins and outs." Great Idea #15 exchanges a life insurance policy for an annuity—more on 1035 exchanges. It's possible to make this transaction tax-free as well. But, you can't exchange an annuity for a life insurance contract and get the same effect.

Great Idea #16 uses annuities to save taxes on Social Security income. This is a little known strategy that the law allows. It's something every retired person should consider.

Great Idea #17 uses annuities to protect serious money for a surviving spouse. There are many applications of this strategy. And, one may be appropriate in your situation.

Great Idea #18 describes how annuities can make legal awards more secure—so-called "structured settlements." If you've won a lawsuit or the lottery or you are entering into a divorce settlement, this strategy is an important option.

Great Idea #19 maximizes family tax savings after an annuitant dies by carefully choosing a policyowner and an annuitant. Of all the tax traps, this looms as truly significant. If you have an annuity policy, check to determine who these parties are to the contract. In most cases, they should be the same.

Great Idea #20 shows how annuities can help you and also provide for those less fortunate via charitable bequests and gift-annuities. This Idea explains why some assets make better charitable gifts than others. You'll also discover why CGIAs are a creative strategy for those charitably inclined.

Great Idea #21 explains how to convert Medicaid accessible resources into inaccessible streams of annuity income. If you have a loved one or friend who is investigating Medicaid nursing home benefits, a carefully structured annuity plan may make qualification easier.

"*If only God would give me some clear sign!*

Like making a deposit in my name in a Swiss bank account."

Woody Allen

Money Magic With Annuities:
Great Ideas for Creative Investors

Table of Contents

1

Create a retirement fund for young children.

"In the long run, a short cut seldom is." Malcolm Forbes

Have you heard the story about the investor who once gave his young grandson, John, a few shares of General Electric? The shares are now worth a million dollars, and now John uses the dividends to supplement his retirement income and help others less fortunate.

You can do something like this for a grandchild or child in the family line. Let's say you gift $10,000 to an irrevocable trust for your new grandson, Tommy. The trustee purchases a single premium deferred annuity. Tommy is the annuitant, and the trust is beneficiary. At a 9 percent rate of return—one double in 8 years, there will be seven doubles by Tommy's age 56 when the annuity contract is worth $1,280,000. Then, it can pay him a 9 percent annual income of $115,200. There is also cash for emergencies along the way, as well as some extra benefits granted to trusts and annuities by our system.

Here are some pointers that will help your planning for Tommy's annuity:

◻ According to 1986 tax law, policy income is taxed currently if a "non-natural" person (a trust) owns an annuity contract. There is an exception if the trustee holds an annuity simply as agent for its beneficiary.

A word of caution: To build an annuity in trust without taxes, closely follow the IRS rules regarding non-natural annuity owners. Obtain good legal advice about this from the lawyer who writes your trust document. Handy references are IRC Sec. 72(u)(1); H.R. Conf. Rep. No. 990841 (TRA); and Letter Rulings, 9204014, 9204010, 9639057, 9752035 and 9810015.

◻ If you want to be Tommy's trustee, you shouldn't be the trustor. Instead, have your spouse create his trust and transfer her money to it.

◻ When Tommy is a minor, only his guardian can make withdrawals from the trust. Your lawyer will probably suggest that Tommy be permitted to demand funds from the trust annuity thereafter. To discourage these distributions, offer incentives not to withdraw. For example, ask counsel about a provision in your will that limits Tommy's other inheritance rights if he withdraws more than, say, 5 percent of the trust principal in any one year before he is in his mid-50s.

◻ When making Tommy's gift, you'll need to give his guardian a limited right (up to 30 days) to withdraw the money. Otherwise, there is a gift tax unless you haven't claimed all of your unified credit exemption amount ($1 million in year 2006, for example).

¤ Instead of an annuity, Tommy's trustee might invest in taxable investments earning 9 percent (6 percent net after taxes)—one double in 12 years, and 4-$\frac{1}{2}$ doubles in the next 54 years. If so, Tommy's $10,000 trust fund will grow to merely $240,000 by his age 55. That's much less than the annuity value of $1,280,000. In addition, someone must manage the investments and pay for the cost of preparing tax returns every year. The annuity just makes much more sense because of its simplicity, tax deferral features, and benefit from the Rule of 72.

¤ If Tommy takes money from the annuity before he is age 59-$\frac{1}{2}$, he'll probably pay an extra 10 percent penalty tax under the law. Before he makes a withdrawal, he should compare four options if he applies 1999 (See Idea #6.) law. These are:

(a) take a series of substantially equal periodic payments over his life expectancy (to avoid the penalty);

(b) take payments selectively in low tax-rate years until 59-$\frac{1}{2}$;

(c) simply take the money and pay the tax; or

(d) wait until 59-$\frac{1}{2}$ to withdraw income from the policy.

2

Create a strong financial base for generations to come.

*"The secret of staying young is to live honestly,
eat slowly, and lie about your age."* Lucille Ball

I believe that most people want to leave a sound values-based financial heritage for their family. It's difficult, however, to do this when you consider the possibilities of estate taxes, long-term care costs, stock market uncertainty, and even the money demands of increased longevity.

Let's say some of the following apply in your situation:

¤ You would like to do something special for future members of your family, even though you will never meet them.

¤ You know how difficult it may be for loved ones to accumulate significant wealth in the future. You want to help matters along since you have the ability to do it.

¤ You want others to receive a check that has your name on it *forever.*

¤ You've already provided for children and a

grandchild, Tommy. Now it's time to help them do something for their offspring.

¤ You'd like to help educate future members of the family.

¤ You'd like to endow an entrepreneur who wants to start a business.

¤ You'd like to leave something for charity and those less fortunate, but not at the expense of future generations.

Let's assume you have about $100,000 to place in a fund dedicated to future generations. Can this really build, say, a $1 million kitty for your grandchildren's children? If so, what's the best way to make the program self-completing?

If you followed conventional wisdom, the results could fall short of what you could achieve with annuities. Here's an example for comparison's sake:

Place $100,000 in mutual funds or securities earning 6 percent after income taxes—one double in 12 years. Let no one touch this until your death in 30 years when everything will be worth about $600,000 (2-$1/2$ doubles). After paying estate taxes @ 50 percent, your children keep $300,000 until they die in about 25 years. By then, the sum will be worth $1.2 million (2 doubles). After subtracting an estate tax of $600,000, your grandchildren re-invest the remains for another 25 years, which grows to $2.4 million (2 more doubles). Then, estate taxes of $1.2 million are subtracted before your great-grandchildren finally inherit the remaining $1.2 million. Mission accomplished—but at the expense of so much time, trouble and taxes. And there isn't any guarantee that the money will be safe in the meantime. Not a very pretty picture when you think about it.

Here's a better way (a grandchild's investment trust)—this approach requires that you set aside only $20,000 instead of $100,000:

Place $20,000 in a trust fund for grandson, Tommy. The trustee makes investments earning 9 percent, which is really 6 percent after taxes. The sum doubles in 12 years. The money accumulates for 85 years (7 doubles) until Tommy dies. At that point, it is worth $2.5 million. After subtracting estate taxes @ 50 percent, there is a $1.25 million kitty for Tommy's children, your great-grandchildren. The good news: You get to the same result by investing merely $20,000 (instead of $100,000). The trust is a much better way to go, because it avoids estate taxes in two generations—yours and your children's—before it reaches Tommy's family.

Here are some planning pointers for Tommy's trust:

¤ Our transfer system intends to tax each estate as it passes from one generation to another. So, you'd think a grandchild's trust naturally owes estate taxes when both you and your children die (and again when Tommy dies). Well, here's how you avoid transfer taxes until this money reaches a great-grandchild:

(a) Make the trust irrevocable;

(b) Limit your gifts to $10,000 annually for

Tommy;

(c) Allow Tommy's guardian up to 30 days to withdraw the gift; (d) Make Tommy sole beneficiary of the trust; and

(e) Have an attorney provide wording in the document that causes trust assets to be included in Tommy's estate tax base when he dies—an IRS requirement. The reference is IRC Sec. 2642(c). (An example is language that permits Tommy to bequeath the trust fund to *anyone!*)

A word of caution: An outright bequest may cause the trust to come to an end. If this alarms you, permit Tommy to bequeath only to creditors. Since he won't do this, the invested cash will be there in trust for Tommy's children. The IRS will be happy, however, because it collects an estate tax anyway.

¤ If your spouse makes the gift, you can be trustee. The children can be trustee after you die.

Here is an even better way. In this example, a grandchild's trust acquires an annuity:

Let's say that instead of investments earning 9 percent (6 percent after taxes), the trustee uses your $20,000 gift to acquire a deferred annuity earning 9 percent—one double in 8 years. With 10-1/2 doubles, it will be worth nearly $30 million at Tommy's age 85. After estate and income taxes of about $24 million,* Tommy's children still will have $6 million.

In other words, for the same $20,000 investment, your great-grandchildren net $6 million instead of the $1.25 million with taxable investments—more than a

350 percent improvement. This illustrates the power of tax-deferred investing, especially over a long period of time.

*Here's the story on the taxes. The estate taxes at 55 percent are enormous—about $16.5 million. Since nearly $12 million of this is deductible against income taxes, they are about $7.2 million—40 percent x $18 million ($30 million less $12 million). The total tax burden is a whopping $23.7 million ($16.5 million + $7.2 million). But after all of these assessments, there still is more than $6 million available for your great-grandchildren. Tax deferral wins in the long run. And there's one more advantage to the annuity—if Congress eventually cancels the income and estate tax, a tax-deferred annuity may become totally tax-free. Why pay these taxes now when you may not have to—ever!

3

Create an education fund for a young child.

*"All work and no play makes jack. With enough jack,
Jack needn't be a dull boy." Malcolm Forbes*

If you are a grandparent, it's natural to help with a formal education for a new-born child. Here's one approach, although it's not what I recommend.

Let's say you gift $10,000 on behalf of a new granddaughter, Laura, under your state's Uniform Gifts to Minors Act. Her parent is custodian; Laura is the annuitant, and her estate is the beneficiary. Assuming investments earn 6 percent after taxes, which doubles the sum in 12 years, this fund will increase to about $25,000 by the time she is 18. Gradually liquidate the fund to pay her tuition and living expenses.

The taxes on Laura's trust income will be paid by her parents until she reaches age 14—a so-called "Kiddie tax." Then, if under state law Laura's parents must support her past age 14, trust income may be taxed to her father and mother until Laura actually becomes an adult. The rules are complicated and good tax advice is important.

There's a simpler and better alternative. Place Laura's $10,000 gift in an education trust for her benefit. The trustee acquires a tax deferred annuity contract that earns 9 percent—one double in 8 years. It accumulates to about $50,000 in 18 years (2-$\frac{1}{4}$ doubles) when it is paid out for her education.

As Laura takes payments from the annuity, she'll pay a 10 percent penalty tax (and the normal income tax as well) on everything above the $10,000 gift. [The tax reference is IRC Sec. 72(q).] Although she'll owe some penalty taxes, there still are advantages to using annuities (vs. taxable investments) to fund a new-born's educational expenses. For instance,

¤ All of the Kiddie tax complications are avoided. And twice the capital is on hand ($50,000 instead of $25,000). Why pay taxes when you don't have to?

¤ Even with a 10 percent surtax, Laura may still pay a low overall tax. For example, for tax years beginning in 1999, a single taxpayer pays federal taxes at a rate of only 15 percent on taxable income up to $25,750. Although the extra 10 percent surtax raises her overall percentage to 25 percent—this still may be less than her parent's rate under the Kiddie tax rules.

¤ When Laura reaches age 18, there may be other family funds available for her education costs and expenses. If so, the annuity can be continued for emergencies and her retirement income need~ Idea #1).

4

An up-and-coming executive or professional compares annuities to an IRA.

"He is a good man whom fortune makes better." Thomas Fuller

Certainly, tax deductible IRAs, 401(ks), pension and profit sharing plans are the cornerstone to a solid retirement strategy. And well they should be.

Here are some of the reasons:

¤ Personal tax deductible contributions save income taxes, and provide an opportunity to reinvest the tax benefits for additional retirement income.

¤ When you contribute to 401(k) or profit-sharing programs (an employer plan), the sponsor may add its allocation to your account too.

¤ Contributions to employer plans are sheltered from a participant's creditors under Federal law, and personal contributions to IRAs are protected as well under the laws of most states.

¤ Earnings on contributions to IRAs and tax qualified employer plans are tax-deferred under the law.

¤ In theory, most retirees are probably in lower

tax brackets when they take their retirement income and finally pay the tax.

Everything considered, IRAs and employer plans offer a nice package of retirement and tax benefits for almost everyone. Annuities, however, can make a great supplement or substitute. Consider this example:

Frank, a successful professional, age 36, wants to set aside $100,000 for retirement at age 60. He inquires about comparing an IRA to a tax deferred annuity and receives this information from his tax adviser:

IRAs vs. Annuities—An Analysis

¤ Deductible contributions to IRAs are normally restricted to $2,000 annually. An employer's deductible contributions to 401(ks), Keoghs and other plans are also limited under law and by the terms of a plan document. In all IRAs and tax qualified employer plans, you are required to begin taking distributions by age 70-$\frac{1}{2}$. (If, however, the law *were* to allow a full $100,000 tax deductible contribution to a tax qualified plan, you'd save $40,000 in income taxes @ a 40 percent rate. If this were invested @ 6 percent net, one double in 12 years, you'd have a real plus— $160,000 of the government's money, two doubles by age 60.)

¤ There are no limits on contributions to annuities. There is no age 70-$\frac{1}{2}$ rule either, that requires you to take taxable distributions from the annuity policy at that time. You just don't get to claim a tax deduction and reinvest the tax savings. Therefore, an annuity offers longer tax-deferral than an IRA or pension fund, and you own a private contract that is free from government forms or restrictions—advantages that may partially make up for the lack of a tax deduction in the beginning.

In summary, contributions to IRAs and employer plans are limited by their provisions and your eligibility to participate in these programs. But, you can invest all you wish in a tax deferred annuity with no age 70-$\frac{1}{2}$ payout requirement. Contribute what you can to tax qualified plans. Then place the remainder in a complementary annuity policy. This combination gives you a unique mixture of deductions, flexibility and tax deferral. You'll be taking advantage of all that our system allows.

5

An entrepreneur sells a business for lifetime income from a private annuity.

"The avoidance of taxes is the only intellectual pursuit that carries any reward." John Maynard Keynes

Here's a common sense explanation of a *commercial* annuity: You pay money to an insurance company in exchange for a lifelong stipend. You can make this arrangement with a person instead, and call it a *private annuity.*

Private annuities usually involve the sale of a business or real estate to family members in exchange for a lifetime income. At death when payments cease, there is nothing left in the seller's estate. Voila! An asset belongs to the next generation without anyone paying a transfer tax. This can really give you some huge estate planning advantages.

The IRS permits private annuities as long as some rules are followed. First, there can be no security to back-up the arrangement. There must be a reasonable probability that the buyer can afford to make your payments. You should also be in good health—and at least expected to live more than a year. Finally, the payments must be calculated according to special tables under the Internal Revenue Code.

Here's an example:

You own a building worth $1 million. Eventually, the estate taxes @ 50 percent may force your family to sell, especially if the property increases in value over the years. You know that a *gift* to your son, Eddie, involves a gift tax. You are also aware that if you keep the cash flow, this "life estate" still causes the property to be included in your estate tax base.

The solution: Obtain a professional appraisal of the building. Then, *sell* Eddie the $1 million property in exchange for a private lifetime annuity—a pre-arranged amount calculated according to IRS tables. If the building increases in value, it won't matter. There is nothing to tax in your estate because there are no more payments after you die.

You'd think everyone would do this. However, the drawback is the large payment tax law requires you to take. It's all based on Treasury's interest rates and how long the IRS expects you to live. *A word of caution:* If your payment is too low, the transaction is treated as a partial gift to your son. This will result in a tax disaster, because the building's value at your death will likely be added to your estate tax-base.

Let's say you are age 65 and anticipate living another 20 years (your IRS life expectancy). When U.S. Treasury interest rates are about 6.5 percent, you sell the $1 million building in exchange for a private lifetime annuity. According to IRS tables, your son must pay you about $116,000 each year.

Actually, you could say this arrangement pays principal plus interest at the hefty rate of about 10 percent per year. (That's the earnings rate which will "liquidate" $1 million with interest over a 20 year period when $116,000 is paid annually—first payment after 12 months.) Of course, Eddie must also pay other business expenses (plus income taxes), before he sends you $116,000 under terms of the sale.

You aren't convinced this is a bad deal, however. You reason that the building should increase in value (but Eddie's payments are fixed in the sales contract) and if you die in say three or four years, Eddie doesn't have to pay anymore. You realize the family will save a bundle in taxes because the building's value is removed permanently from your estate tax base.

As I said before, private annuities can be almost magical in the right circumstances. I suggest considering them if:

¤ You want to "freeze" the value of a business, some real estate or another appreciating asset in your estate;

¤ Due to smoking or poor health, your life expectancy may be subpar;

¤ You come from a family that doesn't outlive the mortality tables;

¤ You own an asset that will provide enough cash to make payments required by the IRS;

¤ You trust the purchaser. Remember, you can't

look to the asset for security if the buyer defaults. You may, however, gift separate funds to help make your payment in a pinch. And you can also insure the payee to assure payments will continue if he or she dies prematurely.

Obviously, there is much to consider in a private annuity transaction. Raise the matter with a financial adviser. Ask for an analysis, and weigh the alternatives. You may decide that private annuities are a profitable addition to your estate plan.

"WE BOTH WIN"

6

Take income from your annuity policy and sidestep an IRS penalty tax.

"If you have ten thousand regulations you destroy all respect for the law." Winston Churchill

You shouldn't acquire an annuity policy as a short-term investment. Here's why:

¤ There may be early surrender charges when you withdraw funds from the policy;

¤ Withdrawals are taxed first (up to your profit) and secondly as a tax-free return of premium; and

¤ All taxable withdrawals are ordinary income and not capital gains.

There may be another reason not to take money from an annuity policy. If you are under 59-$\frac{1}{2}$, Congress discourages annuity payments by imposing a penalizing 10 percent surtax on amounts that represent taxable income. [The reference is IRC, Section 72(q).]

The bad news: Let's say at age 45, you purchase an annuity for $100,000 and surrender it at age 55 for $210,000. You'll pay taxes on $110,000, plus a 10 percent penalty tax of $11,000 (10 percent x

$110,000 of taxable profit). There is no penalty tax on the return of your $100,000 investment.

The good news: A few distributions are protected from the penalty tax. These include payments if you—

¤ are disabled or die; or

¤ take a series of equal amounts over your life expectancy or the joint lives of you and a named beneficiary, using a reasonable method of calculating payments.

It's the series of equal payments exemption that usually allows you to sidestep the penalty tax, and they can be taken at anytime. Here's an example:

Let's say you are 55, and need income from the annuity policy worth $210,000. The premium was $100,000, and according to IRS tables, your lifespan will be 28.6 years. If you presume a 7 percent interest rate over a 28 year period, the sum of $210,000 will pay you $17,300 annually—first payment after 12 months. In other words, $210,000 is the *present value* of $17,300 paid each year for 28 years when 7 percent interest is earned on the unpaid balance.

Now, you have the annual payment—$17,300! (The monthly payment is about $1,400.) What's more—you can stop taking from the policy after five years when you are 60.

These additional pointers will aid your understanding of this strategy. They'll also help you avoid running afoul of the penalty rules.

¤ The payment plan I've described is like a private annuity between you and your policy. With a principal and interest amortization schedule, you calculate a lifetime payment plan using a reasonable life expectancy and an appropriate rate of interest. Then, you must take this payment for *at least* 60 months (and at least until your age 59-$^1/_2$). Any changes (except at your death or disability) will cause assessment of the penalty tax on funds received, plus interest retroactive to when you began the payments.

¤ All payments are taxable as ordinary income as the policy value is gradually reduced to $100,000 in value—the original premium. Then, any additional payments are first interest earned, and secondly a tax-free return of premium. For example, after receiving taxable payments for several years, the policy is reduced from $210,000 in value to $100,000 in 2019. Next year, it earns interest of $5,000. Of your $17,300 payment in 2020, $5,000 is taxable and $12,300 is a tax-free return of premium. In each succeeding year, your tax-free share will increase as the balance of the annuity account is liquidated.

¤ After taking payments for 60 months or until reaching age 59-$^1/_2$, if later, you can modify the payments to fit your particular circumstances. Or, you can stop the payments and the policy will continue accumulating interest on a tax-deferred basis.

¤ As an alternative to this plan, you might annuitize the policy and take lifetime payments according to a schedule provided by the insurance company. The annual payment will be less than $17,300 because the insurer probably will credit less than 7 percent interest when calculating the annuity payment. Since this policy is annuitized, a portion of *each* payment is taxable, and a fixed share is tax-free under the law.[1] Finally, when your payout is set by the insurer, there can be no changes after five years or reaching 59-$\frac{1}{2}$.

In summary, although the law imposes a 10 percent surtax for pre-59-$\frac{1}{2}$ taxable distributions from annuities, it's always possible to arrange a penalty tax-free payment schedule if you follow the rules. In the early years, your payments will be fully taxable; in the later years, the payment will be mostly a tax-free return of your investment. (If you annuitize, however, a fixed portion of each payment over your life expectancy is tax-free.) Once established, the plan cannot be changed (without penalty taxes) until the later of 60 months or your reaching 59-$\frac{1}{2}$.

---

[1] Actually, here's the precise calculation: In this example, you invested $100,000 in the annuity policy. Since your life expectancy is 28.6 years, $3,497 ($100,000 divided by 28.6) of each payment of $17,300 is *tax-free* for the 28.6 year period. The balance of $13,803 is taxable. After 28.6 years, the full payment is taxable.

7

Take an annuity income from your IRA and avoid the minimum distribution rules.

*"Don't gamble! Take all your savings and buy some good stock
and hold it till it goes up, then sell it.
If it don't go up, don't buy it." Will Rogers*

They say that the only bad thing about traditional Individual Retirement Account (IRAs) is taking out your money. You pay ordinary income taxes on minimum required payments, and when you reach 70-$\frac{1}{2}$ you may also pay a 50 percent excise tax on anything you don't take! (For example, let's say you are 70-$\frac{1}{2}$, and the minimum required annual payment is $40,000. You make a calculations mistake and take only $30,000. *The result:* You'll pay ordinary income taxes on the *entire* $40,000—and pay a 50 percent penalty tax of $5,000 (.50 x $10,000), because you didn't take the full $40,000 distribution.

There is one simple way not to run afoul of the IRA minimum distribution rules. Purchase a commercial annuity before the required beginning date (April 1 following the year of attaining age 70-$\frac{1}{2}$).

A life annuity is permissible; you can even have a

policy with a term certain (with or without payments over your *lifetime*). For example, IRS tables assume someone age 70 will live 16 years until age 86. Consequently, you can have (a) a life annuity, (b) a 16 year term certain annuity, or (c) a life annuity with at least 16 annual payments guaranteed.

If you are married, a joint and survivor annuity is allowed. You can have a term certain, also, if you wish. For example, you and your spouse are ages 70 and 66, and IRS tables assume you'll have a combined life expectancy of 22 years. Therefore, with 22 annual payments guaranteed you can have (a) a joint and survivor life annuity, (b) a 22-year term certain annuity, or (c) a joint and survivor life annuity with 22 annual payments guaranteed.

You can even have a joint and survivor life annuity with someone other than a spouse. Here, the joint life expectancy cannot exceed a combination of yours and a beneficiary "presumed" to be 10 years your junior. For instance, if you are 70 and your daughter is 50, your combined life expectancy (26.0 years) is based on ages 70 and 60.

In other words, there is a broad range of annuity income arrangements for an IRA account. Both fixed and variable annuities are permitted, and annuities that have cost-of-living increases qualify, too. Payments must be "non increasing," unless they conform to the IRS regulations.

Here's a suggestion: If you look to your IRA for income but don't want to manage the money, or the minimum distributions, a straightforward fixed annuity may be the answer to this part of your retirement planning. The payments arrive on time each month, and you won't ever have to pay an unexpected 50 percent excise tax at tax time. The reference is Prop. Reg., Sec. 1.401(a)(9)-1.

One last idea: If you need money from an IRA before age 59-1/2, there is a 10 percent penalty tax similar to the extra tax on pre 59-$\frac{1}{2}$ distributions from annuities. (See Idea #6.) The reference is IRC, Sec. 72(t). There are a few exceptions, including payments if you are disabled or die.

For example, let's assume you are 55 and have a IRA worth $200,000. Your life expectancy is 28.6 years. If you assume 7 percent interest, the correct annual payment from the IRA is $17,300. (See Idea #6.) Instead, you can acquire a commercial IRA annuity that pays over a 28.6 year life expectancy.

Either way, you can take IRA distributions without paying the 10 percent extra penalty tax. *A word of caution:* Normally, a commercial annuity won't permit you to switch back to accumulation after taking payments for the minimum period of five years—or age 59-$\frac{1}{2}$ if later. Ask an adviser about the availability of this stop-and-go arrangement.

8

Arrange an **IRA** annuity income to fund a home mortgage loan.

"Anyone who says money doesn't buy happiness doesn't know where to shop." Anonymous

In Idea #7, I describe how someone age 55 can take a series of equal payments from an IRA without paying a 10 percent penalty tax. In Idea #8, I'll show you how to actually cash-in an IRA without paying any taxes. This concept combines an annuity and a home mortgage in a very creative way.

Let's base this example on the following circumstances: You are age 65, and in good health. You expect to live another 20 years, your IRS life expectancy.

¤ You have a $300,000 IRA, and average at least 12 percent earnings on its investments. It is targeted for your family someday. However, you are aware that income and estate taxes could take up to 75 percent of this money before it ever reaches your heirs.

You also wonder about how your beneficiaries will handle the IRA once they receive it. Will your spouse leave it to a new husband? Will your children spend it wisely? If you name a trust beneficiary, must the trustee liquidate the IRA just to pay the taxes? With many issues on the table, you are even considering a cash-in right now. At least you'll have $200,000 or so after paying the income taxes. You could give this to the family or those less fortunate, and everyone could have some real fun for a change.

¤ You also have two homes that are worth about $500,000. These are essentially debt-free, and could be mortgaged for about $375,000. Well, I've set the stage for some interesting financial maneuvering that just may surprise you. Let me explain:

¤ You obtain a $300,000 - 20 year home loan @ 9 percent "interest-only" ($27,000 paid annually-about $2,150 per month). The interest is tax deductible.

¤ Your IRA acquires a $300,000 life-only variable annuity that will pay you $40,000 annually—about $3,200 per month, if it earns a 12 percent rate of return. Your checks continue until death. These payments are fully taxable.

¤ You commit a portion ($27,000 annually) of the variable annuity payment to your mortgage lender. The remainder of $13,000 is sent directly to you. After income taxes @ 33 percent, you net about $9,500 from the annuity payment.

¤ To cover the mortgage loan, you obtain a $300,000 life insurance policy for $8,500 annually. After 20 years, this policy will have cash surrender values of about $150,000.

Eureka! This string of transactions transforms a $300,000 taxable IRA into at least $300,000 tax-free cash in your pocket from the mortgage loan (about 150 percent of the IRA's value if you cashed-out now and paid the taxes). You can spend the money, give it to those less fortunate, reinvest it for retirement income, or just bury it your back yard. You have full control, and there are no more rules or limitations associated with an IRA.

Obviously, you can change these parameters to reflect your situation. For example:

¤ You don't have to use a variable annuity to liquidate the IRA. You can acquire a fixed annuity, but it won't offer the possibility of a 12 percent return. You will, however, have certainty of a guaranteed payment. Or, instead of an annuity, you can arrange each year to withdraw a 12 percent payment directly from the IRA.

¤ Your loan doesn't have to be interest-only. You can amortize principal and interest over a period of time; the payment will be larger, but mostly tax-deductible in the early years; and a lender will probably charge less interest than if you merely pay the interest.

¤ If you gift the insurance policy to your children (or a trust for their benefit), the proceeds may be eliminated from your estate tax base—an added plus.

¤ Of course, you can use a portion of the loan proceeds for extra insurance to benefit family or charity.

¤ You can take some of the loan proceeds to acquire an immediate annuity. A portion of each payment will be taxable, and a fixed share will be tax-free.

¤ Some really good news: If you reinvest the loan money in buy-and-hold investments, any long-term capital gains are taxed @ say 20 percent. That's usually a much lower rate than the ordinary income tax owed someday on your IRA profits! In other words, funds wisely invested outside an IRA may actually perform better than the tax-deferred IRA itself.

9

Use an immediate annuity to cover your fixed living expenses.

"It's hard to believe that some day I'll be an ancestor." Robert Half

Here's a neat little idea that will make your financial life a whole lot easier. Let's say each month you write checks for—

Home mortgage	$1,000
Light, heat and water (averaged)	250
Life Insurance premium	1,450
Health insurance premium	500
Misc. insurance premium	300
Car payment	<u>500</u>
Total	$4,000

And when you consider stamps, envelopes, checking expense and the overall aggravation—you'll probably spend a few hundred dollars of extra wasted cash each year, just to pay your bills. What's more: It appears you'll be paying these amounts for a long time, probably until you die.

Consider these suggestions: Authorize your bank to pay the fixed bills. They'll probably do this automatically without any charge to your account. Then use some ready cash to acquire a single premium immediate annuity. If you are in your 60s, about $500,000 might buy a guaranteed income to cover these expenses as long as you live. Once you have the policy, ask the insurance company to send your annuity check directly to the bank.

¤ A good time to do this financial planning is when there is a windfall—say you receive a modest inheritance, win the lottery, sell a business, or cash-in a sizeable accrued benefit from a tax-qualified retirement plan.

¤ Once the program begins, you can always have the check sent directly to you. The beauty of the bank-annuity arrangement is the time and effort it saves you.

¤ If $500,000 seems like a large amount, be aware that it is simply the present value of these fixed obligations for the rest of your life. You could, of course, cover them for merely a set period, perhaps 10 years. Using a 6 percent interest rate, you'd need to set aside about $380,000.

10

Use an immediate annuity for greater peace of mind.

"A bank is a place where they lend you an umbrella in fair weather and ask for it back again when it begins to rain." Robert Frost

In Idea #9, I describe how to set aside funds in an annuity to pay your fixed living expenses. This makes everyday financial life just a little bit easier.

Immediate annuities are also an intriguing opportunity for successful investors. Let me explain how to integrate a guaranteed fixed immediate annuity into your financial plan.

Let's say you are male in your mid-60s, and a portion of your portfolio consists of $100,000 in liquid cash money market funds. Your financial adviser proposes you place this money in an immediate annuity which (mid-1999) guarantees a payment of $735 monthly for 20 years. The total payout is $176,400 ($735 x 240).

Each year, you'll receive $8,820, and a level amount—$5,000 ($\frac{1}{20}$ of your $100,000 investment) is tax-free. The remainder of $3,820 is taxable, and this nets you about $2,547 after a 33 percent income tax. Your annual after-tax return is $7,547 ($5,000 plus $2,547), and all payments cease after 20 years.

You also receive the following financial analysis to help in your purchasing decision.

How You Compare a 20-Year Fixed Immediate Annuity to Comparable Financial Alternatives

¤ The 20-year annuity happens to provide a *guaranteed* 6 percent return on your money. In other words $100,000 is the *present value* of an income stream of 240 monthly payments—$735 each ($8,820 annually) when principal is liquidated, and 6 percent interest is credited on the unpaid balance.

¤ Since an annuity is taxed under some special rules, a proportionate equal share—$5,000—is a tax-free return of your principal each year. The balance of $3,820 is taxable. If, instead, you loaned $100,000 (at 6 percent interest) to someone who paid you $735 monthly for 20 years, this loan is amortized under a schedule—and most of each payment is taxable interest early on; the annuity payment is better because you'll pay taxes evenly and will be able to reinvest your early tax savings for extra income.

¤ The annuity payment is guaranteed—no more, no less. The insurer sets aside reserves for this, and there is a State Insurance Guaranty Fund to back up everything in the unlikely event of financial trouble. (Most State Insurance Departments will not permit insurance agents to refer to a Guaranty Fund as a reason to buy an annuity. I mention it merely as an educational aide.)

¤ In the mid-90s, the Treasury 30 year, long-term bond is paying 6.05 percent. As an alternative to the 20-year—$735 monthly annuity, it pays $6,050 at the end of each year, or slightly less than $3,025 semi-annually. It is an excellent safe alternative to the annuity. However, you won't receive a check each month, and all payments are taxable. The Treasury bond pays less, but you'll still have your capital at the end of the 20-year term. It will fluctuate in value, and if you cash-out early—it will be worth more if interest rates decline, and less if rates increase. It pays 6 percent interest for 30 years (instead of 20 with the annuity). Finally, the Treasury bond is backed by the U.S. Government, and is considered the safest investment you can make.

A summary: The Treasury long-bond and the annuity are essentially interest-rate (6 percent) equals. Both are considered safe, and each has its own unique features.

¤ There are immediate annuities that provide a *lifetime* income, instead of a payment for a fixed period. For example, at age 65, a male can invest (mid-1999) $100,000 in a single premium immediate annuity that guarantees $809 monthly for life—$9,708 each year. This payment is $74 ($809 less $735) more than the 20 year policy. Since your IRS life expectancy is 20 years (male, age 65), $5,000 is tax-free as with the 20-year annuity; the balance of $4,708 is taxable. After paying income taxes @ 33 percent, you'll have net cash flow of about $8,139.

Under the law, all payments are taxable once you've received a return of the original principal of $100,000.

The bad news: You must live about 18 years to receive the same value that is guaranteed under the 20-year fixed period annuity ($9,708 x 18 = $174,740) vs. ($8,820 x 20 = $176,400). *The good news:* If you live longer than 18 years, the life annuity is better and the payments just keep coming. *The bottom line:* With a life annuity, there is the risk of dying too soon. But with the 20 year plan, there is a risk of outliving the payments. Simply put: Take advantage of the system by choosing the best available annuity based on your health, lifestyle and financial circumstances.

¤ If you come from a family that outlives the mortality tables, a life annuity may be an attractive investment. Consider how the following analysis can work to your advantage:

Rates of Return Based on the Number of Years You Live

Male, age 65, $100,000 Single Premium Life Annuity Paying $809 monthly ($9,708 over 12 Months)

If You Live	Total Payout	Equivalent Rate of Interest on Unpaid Balance
10 years, 3 mos.	$ 99,507	0%
18 years	$174,744	6-1/4%
20 years	$194,160	7-1/2%
25 years	$242,700	8-1/2%
30 years	$291,240	9%
35 years	$339,780	9-1/4%

The bottom line: If you live 35 years until age 100, a total payout of $339,780 is equivalent to earning 9-¼ percent interest (on the unpaid balance) guaranteed over 35 years. And that's not a bad rate of return.

$$\neq$$

¤ If the prospect of guaranteed income over a long period of time interests you, you can add some features to balance a life-only immediate annuity program with other investments. For instance,

(a) Use a portion of your cash for a life annuity that also guarantees payments for 20 years. Your monthly income per $100,000 of single premium will be about $7,000—not much less than the 20 year fixed period annuity.

(b) Choose a joint and survivor life annuity that merely pays over two lifetimes. If your wife is, say, age 62, this also pays about $7,000 per month.

(c) To hedge against inflation, use a variable annuity. The payments will fluctuate based on investment performance, but you'll still receive a check each month for life or for a specific period. And hopefully, each payment is more than the last one.

(d) If your health is impaired, ask an insurance agent to obtain quotes from carriers specializing in "impaired risk" immediate annuities. The payout rates will be better.

(e) Some immediate annuities are linked to what

the insurance company earns on its investments. If it earns more, you'll get more income; but you'll always receive the guaranteed payout as a minimum. Ask your financial adviser about these policies.

In summary, immediate annuities offer guaranteed (a) lifetime income (life annuities) (b) income for a fixed period, or (c) a combination of (a) and (b). Fixed annuities promise a specific payment, and variable annuities offer the possibility of enhanced amounts. A professional planner will obtain the best rates and advise on how to mix and match immediate annuities and coordinate them with your other investments.

11

Using annuities and life insurance to enhance income and family capital— an alternative to CDs, Treasuries and bonds.

"Growing old isn't so bad when you consider the alternative."
Maurice Chevalier

As people approach senior status, their tolerance for risk usually decreases. Investments of choice become CDs, Treasuries and even high-grade corporate bonds. This combination can be easily structured to provide safe income streams and liquidity in cash of a financial emergency. Most retirees also want to preserve principal for their heirs. The CD-Treasury-bond approach assures this, if only there is enough income to avoid spending the principal too.

There actually is a safer and better way to position assets for you and your family. It combines immediate annuities and life insurance in interesting ways. Let me explain.

Example: You are in your mid-60s and have a $500,000 CD-Treasury-bond program that pays 6 percent interest—$30,000 annually. After taxes of 33 percent, your net income from this arrangement is about $20,000. In Idea #10, I described an immediate life-only annuity that paid-out $9,708 annually ($8,139 after taxes) in exchange for a $100,000 single premium. Using that example, you'd receive $40,695 (5 x $8,139) after taxes, if the single premium was $500,000. This is $20,695 ($40,695 less $20,000) more than what is provided by your CD-Treasury-bond combination. The annuity concerns you, however, because it "spends" the funds you want your children to have some day.

My suggestions: If you are in good health, it's possible at age 65 to obtain a $500,000 life insurance policy in exchange for a level annual premium of about $12,500. This "replaces" the $500,000 you presently have invested. *The bottom line:* An annuity-insurance program gives you these financial consequences—

¤ You add $20,695 ($40,695 less $20,000) of annual cash flow.

¤ However, if you choose to insure a $500,000 inheritance for the children, your cash flow is reduced by $12,500 in insurance premiums.

¤ *The net result:* You increase your net cash flow by $8,195 ($20,695 less $12,500). That's over 40 percent more than $20,000 offered by the CD-Treasury-bond combination.

Here are some additional planning pointers to consider:

¤ The annuity also lowers your taxable income to $14,305 ($30,000 less $15,695), and your income tax bracket may even be less, as well. The income taxes on Social Security checks may also be less. (See Idea #16.) Finally, an annuity payment is received smoothly the same day each and every month, and it's guaranteed.

¤ You can choose to pay a single premium for the insurance policy as well. You could even purchase two fixed annuities and have one pay annual premiums directly to the life insurance carrier. Or, a fixed annuity can pay the premium and a variable annuity can provide for your personal cash flow.

¤ If you want more for your family, take some of the excess cash flow from the annuity and acquire more life insurance.

¤ Since the annuity plan actually increases your cash flow, you can choose instead, to put less into the annuity. This leaves some emergency funds in your CD-Treasury-bond program.

¤ If you are concerned about liquidity, design an annuity-insurance plan with less, say one-half of your $500,000 in CDs, Treasuries and bonds. The remainder can form a quality emergency fund.

¤ Since any well conceived annuity-insurance combination should improve one's overall financial circumstances, consider placing some of your funds in less conservative investments—perhaps mutual funds, securities or real estate.

¤ Over the years, there are cash values in the insurance policy. Since you can easily borrow them from the insurer, they serve as a source of ready cash in an emergency. This should reduce your concern about lack of liquidity with the annuity-insurance plan.

¤ There is yet another advantage to the annuity-insurance program. By placing the life insurance policy in an irrevocable trust, it can be removed from your estate tax base. Since payments from the annuity cease at death, you've replaced potentially taxable funds with insurance that is fully tax-free.

¤ Finally, consider investing any extra cash flow in a long-term care insurance policy. Or you might choose to gift it to family or those less fortunate.

In short, the pros of the annuity-insurance plan should almost always outweigh its cons. If you work out the details with a financial adviser, you should become more comfortable with the math that's involved. Then, it's just a matter of fitting everything into your circumstances.

12

Managing an irrevocable trust (ILIT) using annuities and life insurance.

"If we command our wealth, we shall be rich and free;
if our wealth commands us, we are poor indeed." Edmund Burke

It's popular to use ILITs to fund life insurance for estate tax liquidity and to replace assets gifted to those less fortunate. Typically, someone creates an ILIT and makes $10,000 annual cash-gifts to the trustee. Presently, there is no gift tax to pay on these transfers as long as trust beneficiaries have a limited time to withdraw the money. These are affectionately called Crummey trusts and are named after a California taxpayer who did battle with the IRS in the 1970s and won.

Let's assume you are age 65, and an ILIT applies for a $1 million insurance policy on your life. Premiums are paid each year with cash gifts of $25,000. At your death, the insurance proceeds aren't part of your estate tax base. If your estate tax rate is 50 percent, you could say $1 million paid to an ILIT is equivalent to $2 million of personal assets subject to transfer taxes.

There are some drawbacks to Crummey trusts, however. For example, it's possible that someone will actually withdraw their gift. At the every least, you'll probably have to have a meeting each year to explain why your children should leave the gifts in the trust.

You can make matters a lot simpler by funding life insurance premiums with an annuity. Here's how:

Example: Instead of making gifts each year and giving notices to withdraw the cash, you simply make a one-time cash gift to the $25,000 trust. The trustee pays the first insurance premium and a single premium for an immediate annuity that pays 19 annual premiums directly into the life insurance policy. Using 6 percent interest your gift will be $304,000 ($25,000 plus about $279,000).

Here are a few planning pointers:

¤ It should be possible (late-1999 rates) to obtain an insurer's guarantee that a $279,000 single premium will pay $25,000 annually for 19 years beginning one year from now.

¤ Your financial adviser will arrange for the annuity insurer to send premiums directly to your life insurance company.

¤ At 65, your life expectancy is 20 years. But it's possible you'll still be alive and owe premiums at age 85.

¤ If you die during the 20 years, any remaining annuity checks are available to your family.

¤ Of course, your trustee can reduce the annuity's

single premium by acquiring a life-only annuity. You'll have to compare paying the premiums for 20 years *and beyond,* to the risk of losing any remaining annuity payments if there is a premature death.

¤ The one-time gift of $304,000 is a taxable gift. However, it is sheltered from taxes if you haven't gifted your lifetime exemption ($1 million in 2006) under the law.

¤ If you don't feel comfortable parting with $304,000, consider gifting less and using an immediate annuity to pay premiums for less than 20 years.

13

For more income, split an annuity premium between two policies.

"The income tax has made liars out of more Americans than golf." Will Rogers

Let's say your goal is more spendable income. You have $100,000 in cash that can be invested in a 10-year CD, Treasury, bond arrangement (a "CD" plan) that pays 6 percent interest. Here's what you'll receive if interest is paid at year end. After income taxes @ 33 percent, you'll have about $4,000 (.67 x $6,000 interest). On the other hand, if interest is paid monthly, you'll gross $488—a total of $5,856 over the year, and about $3,904 after taxes. This brings you net cash of $39,040 over a 10 year period.

There is another possibility, and it combines two annuity policies—a deferred and an immediate contract—into what financial planners call a "split annuity." Here's how you do it. Using the same $100,000 cash,

¤ You invest $56,000 in a deferred annuity that earns 6 percent interest over a 10 year period. *The result*: Your policy will be worth about $100,000 after a decade.

¤ With the remaining $44,000, you acquire a 10 year immediate annuity that also pays 6 percent on the unpaid balance. *The result:* You'll receive a monthly income of $488 ($5,856 over 12 months)—($58,560 over 10 years)—the same amount provided by the CD. But there's a major difference:

With the CD plan, all of your $58,560 in interest income is taxable. With the immediate annuity, only the profit portion of $14,560 ($58,560 less $44,000 invested) is taxed. *The result:* The split annuity arrangement pays the same amount ($58,560), but over 10 years it puts $53,707 [$44,000 plus .6667 ($14,560)] in your pocket. And that's $14,715 more than $39,040 under the CD program.

The bottom line: Over a 10-year period, the split annuity saves you $14,715 in income taxes and the deferred annuity share builds back your original investment kitty of $100,000—another example of money magic using annuities. (See "A Comparison" following this Great Idea.)

It's helpful to consider these additional planning pointers:

¤ If you are interested in stock market-like returns, invest the deferred portion in a variable annuity policy that offers equity investments which fluctuate in value.

¤ If your goal is increasing income at a future date, alter the split. For example, invest say $33,000 in the immediate annuity. When you consider taxes, this keeps your present cash flow about the same as the fully taxable CD program. Then, if you put $67,000 in a deferred annuity, you'll have extra income later on.

¤ When you invest in a deferred annuity, you'll eventually owe taxes when cashing in the policy. However, ask a financial planner about splitting the policy once more when it builds back to $100,000.* For example in 1998, a policyowner made an exchange of a deferred annuity into two separate policies. Although the IRS didn't think this was a tax-free exchange, a court disagreed.*

> *Once the above deferred annuity grows to $100,000, you might (a) transfer $56,000—the original deferred annuity single premium—into a new immediate annuity, and (b) keep deferring the profit of $44,000 in the original contract. This gives you a second split annuity that pays over a period of time measured by your particular facts and circumstances.

In summary

Split annuities take advantage of the system by combining deferred and immediate annuities to give you an improved financial position. Ask your financial planner for a proposal. You'll like what you see.

A Comparison

The CD, Treasury, bond Program	The Deferred-Immediate Annuity Combination —*a Split Annuity*
$100,000 Invested	$100,000 Invested
	(a) $56,000 is put into a deferred annuity earning 6 percent; It grows to $100,000 after 10 years.
$100,000 always on hand; @ 6 percent interest, you receive $488 per month—a total of $58,560 over 10 years.	(b) $44,000 is put into an immediate annuity earning 6 percent interest. It pays $488 per month—a total of $58,560 over 10 years.
After taxes of $19,520 (one third of $58,560), your net income over 10 years is $39,040.	After taxes of $4,853 (one third of $14,560), your net income over 10 years is $53,707.

14

Exchange an old annuity for a new annuity tax-free.

"Be awful nice to 'em goin' up, because you're gonna meet 'em all comin' down." Jimmy Durante

Let's say that in a period of declining interest rates, you own an annuity policy with ABC Insurance Co. There are no surrender charges, and the interest rate is just lowered to 5 percent when other policies are paying more. XYZ Insurance Co. offers a policy paying 7 percent. You decide to cash-in the ABC policy and replace it with a new XYZ contract, even though XYZ does charge if you make an early withdrawal.

There is one possible stumbling block, however. You paid $100,000 for the ABC policy, and it's now worth $200,000. You don't want to pay income taxes on the profit.

Fortunately, there is a solution. Make a tax-free exchange of the old policy for another one. Here's how:

Assign ABC's policy to XYZ Co. in exchange for the higher interest paying contract. Then, XYZ Co. surrenders your ABC policy. As long as the XYZ and ABC policies have identical features, the law makes this a fax-free exchange. The reference is IRC Sec. 1035(a)(3).

What are these identical features? A reasonable reading of tax law indicates that—

¤ The annuitant and owner must be the same. I recommend, also, that the beneficiary—at least initially, be the same as well.

¤ It's best to assign the entire ABC policy to XYZ Co. (Although one court has disagreed with the IRS, their position is that you cannot merely assign some of the money from one annuity into a new policy.) And, if there is an existing policy loan, repay it before making the transfer.

¤ The maturity or retirement dates on each policy must be the same. For example, if ABC Co. requires that you take an income by age 85, the XYZ policy should also commence your income by that date:

Do not cash-in your ABC Co. policy and endorse ABC's check to XYZ Co. The only safe way to make this transaction tax-free is the assignment approach that I've described.

Some words of caution: (1) If you acquired the ABC annuity policy before 1-19-85, and another person is the annuitant, it can be continued until he or she dies. Unfortunately, if you exchange it for XYZ's policy and die before the annuitant, the new contract can't be continued indefinitely; it must be annuitized, or surrendered within five years of your death. In this situation, therefore, I suggest you keep the existing contract because of its greater potential for tax deferral. (2) If you receive a deferred annuity as part of a distribution from a terminating profit sharing or pension plan, it will have some restrictions as to transferability, spousal consent and minimal distributions; if you exchange it for another annuity, the successor policy must have similar provisions. (3) Even though an exchange is tax-free, you may receive a Form 1099R from the first company. There must be a Code 2 in Box 7 of this form to establish that the exchange is tax-free. If not, ask your agent to request a new form. (4) Finally, a new insurer should seek your premium cost basis from the former carrier. If, instead, the second company sets up the *transferred funds* as your basis in the new contract, you'll need to keep good records. Here's why: Eventually when someone annuitizes or surrenders the policy (or withdraws funds form it), your basis in any series of tax-free exchanges is always based on the original premium.

15

Exchange a life insurance policy for an annuity tax-free.

"A nickel ain't worth a dime anymore." Yogi Berra

In Idea #10, I describe how to exchange one annuity for another policy on a tax-free basis. It's also possible to trade a life insurance contract for an annuity without paying taxes on the profit in your present policy. (Apparently, it's even possible to trade *two or more* insurance contracts for only one annuity policy.) Let's say you've paid ABC Insurance Company a total of $105,000 for an insurance policy— and $5,000 covered waiver of premium and double indemnity; the net premiums are $100,000! The cash value is $120,000. On surrender of the policy, therefore, you'd pay taxes on a profit of $20,000 ($120,000 less $100,000 in net premiums).

By converting ABC's policy into an annuity with ABC Co. (or by assigning the contract to another insurer who makes the conversion), you defer taxes on any profit until the annuity policy is surrender or annuitized. For example, if you cash-in the annuity later when it is worth $200,000, the taxable profit is

$100,000 ($200,000 less $100,000), the net premiums in the old insurance policy.

A word of caution: Don't surrender the insurance policy and acquire an annuity with the cash. That makes the $20,000 profit taxable. It's best to use an assignment procedure and let a new insurance company deal with your former carrier. Ask your insurance adviser how to make the exchange correctly. There is some paperwork but it's not a difficult procedure.

Here's an idea that you'll find interesting. Let's assume your insurance policy has a "loss;" you've paid net premiums of $100,000 (your basis) and the cash value is only $70,000. If you surrender it, there is no deduction for a loss on your tax return. However, if you exchange it for an annuity, your basis in the insurance policy becomes the annuity's basis. The result: Over the next few years, growth in the annuity policy (up to a total value of $100,000) is sheltered from income taxes. In effect, the first $30,000 of annuity cash value is *tax-free*—a great example of money magic in action!

Another word of caution: Don't cancel any life insurance without a professional analysis of your family's insurance needs. Be absolutely sure the extra death benefit no longer plays a role in your overall financial planning.

16

Use a deferred annuity to shelter a Social Security check from income taxes.

"The taxpayer: Someone who works for the government but doesn't have to take a civil service examination." Ronald Reagan

Before 1994, Social Security benefits were either not taxable, or a maximum of 50 percent of these payments was countable for income tax purposes. It was relatively easy to compute this taxable amount, if any, with a worksheet and a pocket calculator.

Now, more of your Social Security check is taxable and it's somewhat difficult to make the analysis. In essence, there are five different calculations to make before you determine just how much you'll pay in tax on your Social Security benefits.

The key is understanding a term of art called "provisional income." Basically, this is your adjusted gross income (AGI) *plus* tax exempt interest, *plus* 50 percent of your Social Security benefits). Once provisional income exceeds $25,000 (a single taxpayer) or $32,000 (married taxpayers filing jointly), tax is due on up to 50 percent of your Social Security benefits. For example, if you are single and your provisional income (including $4,000 from $8,000 in Social Security benefits) is $28,000, you'd pay taxes on $1,500 received from the Social Security Administration).*

But, if your provisional income exceeds $32,000 (a single taxpayer), or $44,000 (married taxpayers filing jointly), you'll pay tax on potentially 85 percent of your Social Security benefits.

Determining exactly how much tax is due will probably require a conference with your tax adviser. But one thing is certain: Congress has decided that most of us should include Social Security payments in our "taxable income" base.

Here's where tax-deferred annuities can help. By eliminating or reducing taxable income or tax exempt interest in the equation, it reduces the amount of provisional income on your tax return. Let's say you replace municipal bonds or certificates of deposits with tax deferred annuity contracts. The accrued income in the policy doesn't count as provisional income, and you will gain financially as follows:

¤ There are no current taxes on the annuity profit as it builds up, and

¤ You may save the taxes on most of your Social Security income because its tax deferred interest is not included within the definition of provisional income.

*Here's how the taxable amount is calculated. It is *the lesser of* (a) one-half your Social Security benefit (.50 x $8,000), or (b) one-half of your provisional income over $25,000 (.50 x $3,000). Applying this test, (a) is $4,000 and (b) is $1,500. You'll pay taxes on $1,500.

Indeed, these tax savings possibilities are intriguing. Of course, this switch requires some financial maneuvering since there will be a reduction in your current cash-flow. (Annuities accumulate interest; bonds pay interest currently.) However, it may be possible to gain back this money by spending invested capital while the annuity is accumulating interest. In other words, deplete some other asset in an amount equal to the policy's build-up.

Work closely with a financial adviser. Using annuities to shelter Social Security benefits from taxes can really help in the right circumstances.

17

Protect some serious money for a surviving spouse.

"A fool and her money are soon courted." Helen Rowland

It's natural to provide for family in the event of our disability or death. That's why we don't completely use some of our investments and insurance during our lifetimes.

Here's a story about how one fine gentleman assured some special financial security for his second wife, Mary, age 67. I'll call him Jonathan, age 70.

There were some matters that concerned him greatly. He didn't want children (from previous marriages) to go after any of the money he left to his second wife. He even worried that she might face similar pressure from a new husband, if she remarried. And he knew that Mary didn't have much experience with investments, so he wanted to make money management easier for her as well.

The solution: With $300,000, Jonathan acquired an immediate joint life annuity that paid them $2,000 per month. He directed that all payments be sent directly to their joint bank account.

Here's what Jonathan accomplished for both of them:

◻ He assured a guaranteed return of more than 8 percent annually ($24,000 paid over the course of a year) for their lifetimes—22 years according to IRS tables. This could provide a payout of $528,000 ($24,000 x 22) if either of them lived the period. Since they were in reasonably good health, they might even receive more if at least one of them beat the odds and lived beyond the 22 years.

◻ Since the arrangement was irrevocable, there was no possibility family members or even creditors could obtain funds transferred to the insurance company.

◻ Jonathan and Mary had a $2,000 base monthly income for their financial well being. *More important:* It would be there for Mary if she survived him, and she wouldn't need to have anyone manage investments behind the money.

◻ Jonathan's other assets were freed for Mary and their families. He could even leave more to children at his death because of her guaranteed base income.

Here's some other possibilities:

◻ Jonathan could arrange the annuity to pay more while they are both alive—and less thereafter. For example, a single premium of $300,000 might provide $2,500 monthly during both lifetimes, with a reduction to $1,250 per month for the survivor—a so-called joint and 50 percent survivor life annuity.

¤ Or, for a $300,000 single premium, their $2,000 annuity could be paid merely for Jonathan's lifetime, with 240 months assured. This policy wins if Jonathan and Mary both die within 20 years. However, the joint and survivor program is better if either is alive at that time.

18

A structured settlement using annuities—when you win a lawsuit.

"More people should learn to tell their dollars where to go instead of asking them where they went." Roger W. Babson

Congratulations! You win a lawsuit or the lottery! Or, you may score a nice lump sum settlement in a divorce.

These are situations where a lump sum can be paid to the party entitled to an award. As an alternative, annuities can provide structured settlements to guarantee payments over significant period of time.

Here are two examples:

¤ Mary Richardson wins a $6 million lottery. She is informed, however, that if she wants cash, she'll get only $3 million—before income taxes, of course. If she takes the $6 million, it will be at the rate of $300,000 annually for a period of 20 years—a structured settlement using an annuity guaranteed by an insurance company.

¤ Julie Morgan, age 10, wins a lawsuit entitling her to $2.5 million. Instead, the defendant offers a structured payment award as follows:

(a) $100,000 for each of the next 20 years.

(b) An extra $100,000 for her education at age 18.

(c) $500,000 at age 25.

(d) A lifetime income of $125,000 annually beginning at her age 30.

(e) A negotiated cash payment to her family if she dies during the next 20 years.

Annuities are used to fund the obligation. Of course, everything is negotiable. For example, if Mary's family wants to assume some risk, a variable policy could pay more depending on the performance of its investments.

There are a number of tax and estate planning issues associated with all structured settlements. For example:

¤ Can Mary eventually change the designated beneficiary of any payments made after her death?

¤ Will the arrangement create an estate tax obligation at Mary's death? For instance, the present value of the remaining annuity payments will be included in her estate tax base. If so, the settlement should probably provide a cash lump sum to pay these taxes.

¤ When estate taxes are an issue, it may be possible to reduce the size of Mary's estate by allocating a portion of the award to her family. However, if they aren't legally entitled to damages, any payments to them may be a taxable gift by Mary.

19

A tax deferred annuity continues for a surviving spouse.

"An income tax form is like a laundry list—either way you lose your shirt." Fred Allen

You are married and are about to purchase an annuity policy. Some decisions must be made about policyowner, annuitant and beneficiary. Let's review who these parties to the contract are:

The policyowner: This person can add-to, cash-out, change the beneficiary and manage everything to do with the policy.

The annuitant: The life expectancy of this person governs the payout if you annuitize the policy. Naturally, payments are greater if he or she is older (and is expected to die sooner rather than later).

The beneficiary: This person controls and owns the policy when someone dies. For instance, if owner and annuitant are the same, there can be one beneficiary. If different, there probably should be two beneficiaries—one if the owner dies and one if the annuitant dies.

In considering an annuitant, some insurers have a maximum age of 75 or 80. If a policyowner's age exceeds the limit, it is customary to name a second person (a younger spouse or other relative) as the annuitant.

If you own this policy and say your spouse, Mary, is the annuitant, be aware of some tax traps in the law. Let's say Mary (the mere annuitant) dies first and a lump sum becomes payable on December 10th. A beneficiary has 60 days from that date to annuitize and spread-out the income tax bill on the profit. Otherwise, any taxes are due at once.

However, if you (the policyowner) die, it's different. For marrieds, whenever a policyowner-spouse dies, under the law the survivor (a beneficiary-spouse) may elect to step-into-the former owner's shoes and continue the annuity policy. (This can be done when the deceased was policyowner-annuitant or merely a policyowner.) *The result:* There is a potential for continued tax deferral at least until the survivor dies.

My recommendation: In most cases, one spouse should be both policyowner and annuitant. This way, the survivor always has an option to maintain the policy's tax deferral until he or she dies. (Alternately, if one spouse is annuitant and the other married is owner, the policy matures if the annuitant dies first. Here, the survivor already owns the policy and cannot exercise any step-into-the-shoes option. He or she must annuitize or promptly cash-out—and the accumulation phase is automatically over, an inferior tax planning consequence.) Is all of this really just legal gobble-degook? Perhaps, but all consumers interested in annuities (and their advisers) should master these complicated parts of the tax law. Otherwise, there could be some surprises down the road.

20

Charitable tax planning with annuities.

"Make all you can, save all you can, give all you can." John Wesley

If you are interested in benefitting those less fortunate, there are several annuity planning strategies that present win-win opportunities for creative investors and their families. Here are two that involve annuity policyowners and annuitants:

Donating annuity policies to charities.

Let's say you have an annuity policy worth $200,000 purchased 10 years earlier for $100,000. The beneficiary is your son, Bobby, and there are no plans to annuitize this policy before your death. In your will, there is a $200,000 bequest of securities to a favorite charity. They cost you $100,000.

A suggestion: Modify your plan by naming the charity beneficiary of the annuity contract. Then, change your will to bequeath the securities to Bobby when you die. Here's why:

If you leave the annuity to your son, he'll pay income taxes on profit in the policy. If he receives the securities, however, there is no income tax to pay on their appreciation up to your death. Perhaps this is a quirk in the law, but it's just one example of how creative thinking can maximize capital for others—if we take time to plan our affairs correctly.

Entering into a private annuity with your favorite charity.

In Idea #5, I discussed how to transfer assets to family members in exchange for a private annuity. It's also possible to do this with a charitable organization,—and it's called a charitable gift immediate annuity (CGIA).

Let's say you are age 65 and with $100,000 in cash you could acquire an immediate life-only annuity paying about $10,000 per year. Instead, you donate this to charity in exchange for a CGIA, that pays about $7,000 annually.

Obviously, a CGIA pays less than the commercial annuity policy. However, a CGIA also gives you a tax deduction for $30,000—about one-third of your $100,000 gift. And, if you gift an appreciated asset, you'll also avoid paying capital gains taxes on a portion of your profit in the property.

Once you make the CGIA arrangement with a charitable institution, they may "reinsure" their commitment by acquiring a commercial policy to pay you the annuity. This enables the institution to use any remaining cash (about $30,000) immediately for its charitable purposes.

Ask a financial planner to make some calculations regarding CGIAs for your benefit. If you want to help those less fortunate and benefit personally in the process, a CGIA is simple, straightforward and to the point—another example of money magic when you use annuities as part of the equation.

21

Use an annuity in Medicaid financial planning.

"The point to remember is what the government gives it must first take away." John S. Coleman

Some day, you or a family member may question whether Medicaid covers their nursing home expenses. You may even find it necessary to investigate this matter for an elderly parent, relative or a friend.

I'd like to introduce you briefly to some Medicaid qualification rules. I will discuss what happens to the resources and income of two marrieds when one spouse becomes Medicaid eligible. Finally, I'll show you how annuities may soften the blow financially when everything seems hopeless.

Let's assume that Harry and Mary are married, and Harry is a candidate for Medicaid. If he enters the nursing home, he'll be the "institutionalized spouse." Mary is the stay-at-home or "community spouse."

Medicaid eligibility

Medicaid is a welfare program, and Harry must be nearly financially destitute. To become *eligible,*

¤ He is credited with a few exempt assets, including a car and his home.

¤ He has a non-exempt asset limit of perhaps $4,000.

¤ His monthly income limit is say, $1,500. (Once he qualifies, he can only keep a small income for his basic personal needs.)

¤ Mary can have a so-called community spouse capital resource allowance (CSRA)–presume $80,000. If she is broke, Harry can transfer this directly to her.

¤ The law permits Mary to have an unlimited income (pensions, Social Security, etc.). However, if she is poor, the law allows her a Minimum Monthly Maintenance Needs Allowance (MMMNA) that is calculated by a local county agent. Then, if there is any shortfall, she is entitled to some of Harry's personal income– ahead of Medicaid and his nursing home. For example, assume she receives a monthly pension of $800 and Harry has exactly $1,500. If her MMMNA is $2,000, she can have $1,200 from Harry. Then, Medicaid takes the balance of his income.

Harry's Medicaid planning

Let's say Harry has a monthly income of merely $1,500, and it appears he is eligible for Medicare benefits. However, he has $384,000 in non-exempt resources. Therefore, if Mary has no countable assets, he transfers $80,000 (their CSRA) to her. The result: Although he can keep $4,000, he must spend-down

$300,000 of their remaining assets before he qualifies for benefits. He'll be assessed a period of ineligibility as well because these assets exceed their CSRA under the law.

Annuities in Medicaid financial planning.

If Harry transfers $300,000 to a single premium immediate annuity payable to Mary, in most states this sum is removed from their countable resources. And since Mary can have unlimited income, the stream from the annuity belongs to her– and not Harry's nursing home. The argument: Harry and Mary convert a countable resource ($300,000) into non–countable income for her. Harry also qualifies for Medicaid, and there is no period of ineligibility.

The "asset to annuity" strategy must be carefully managed, or Harry will still encounter some period of Medicaid ineligibility. Here are some helpful pointers that help when Medicaid planning becomes an important part of your financial well being:

¤ At present in 1999, it appears most of the states permit the asset-to-annuity planning strategy. However, at least two states count some portion of the annuity's single premium as a countable resource.

¤ An accumulation annuity will be counted as a resource. Only a payout annuity can be used for planning purposes.

¤ The annuity contract must be "actuarially sound." For example, if Mary is age 65 and her Medicaid life expectancy is 15.35 years, the policy should not have a term certain of more than 15 years.

¤ A payout annuity should be finalized before the application for Medicaid is filed. Since all states allow a 30-60 day free-look to cancel annuity and insurance policies, this period should be over as well.

¤ Not all annuity policies qualify for Medicaid planning strategies. For example, the policy should specifically be *non-transferable and irrevocable*. And since the policy should be annuitized prior to submitting a Medicaid application, the insurer should not impose a time limit between acquisition and annuitization. Finally, the policy shouldn't permit a term certain that exceeds a payee's lifespan. Life-only policies should use Medicaid's life expectancy tables to calculate their payouts. In other words, it's important to acquire Medicaid annuities from insurance companies whose contracts carefully conform to the Medicaid rules and regulations.

¤ Finally, Medicaid is always changing the rules. And as this is being written, the press reports that organized crime is skimming hundreds of millions annually from Medicare and Medicaid. Look for some tightening of the rules over the next year or so.

¤ It is crucial to work closely with a financial planner and lawyer who are familiar with your state's Medicaid Administrative Agency. A mistake can be expensive, and good advice is at a premium. Be proactive and select a quality adviser team committed to your best interests. Then, make a sound annuity strategy part of your family's overall financial and estate plans.

Afterword

Now, you've learned some of the magical applications for annuities. Dick Duff has explored the uncommon ground of planning possibilities and expanded strategic options advisors can choose when applying annuity products to challenging financial situations. The results significantly enhance and benefit the financial well being of many consumers.

So what's in store for the future within the marketplace? That is an interesting question but one I am eager to answer. Here's why. For what seems a long time, annuities have been an ultra conservative low interest rate, monthly income retirement product. However, today's policies have broken through these traditional cobwebs and become a proud member of the honor roll of competitive investment and savings vehicles.

Today's annuities are sold by virtually everyone. Not only can you buy them from bankers, brokers, and insurance agents but you can even purchase annuity contracts on television and the Internet. Don't be surprised if your accountant and attorney solicit you for annuities some day. Your local credit union will offer them too— and yes, even the credit card companies. Annuity policies will certainly become a major tool in our everyday financial lives.

Don't be surprised if there is a whole new array of products in the near future such as the first FDIC insured bank CD annuity or a product which combines long term care protection with all of the annuity income tax advantages. You'll even see policies which have stock market, foreign market, and special equity options. This is just the right time for consumers and annuities— a magical combination, also, when you think about it.

Tyrone Clark, President, *Broker's Choice of America,* Denver, Colorado

Epilogue

In *Money Magic* I've stressed the importance of having valued advisers. If a financial planner or insurance broker gave you this book, it's surely an indication that he or she is interested in you and believes in state-of -the-art planning. Give your benefactor a plus and ask for more information.

It's true, also, that not all insurance companies are the same. *First,* it's important that your annuity contract has solid financial backing. Ask your adviser how the carrier is rated by Best's, Standard and Poors, Moody's and Duff and Phelps. *Secondly,* your insurance carrier should be innovative when it comes to the design of its annuity products. Look for new features and policy "extras" that benefit and protect you and your beneficiary.

I'd like to give you (or your financial planner) a roster of insurance companies that are uncommonly creative when it comes to interesting annuity policies. It also contains my description of their unique and up-to-date product features and options. If you are considering a new annuity, I'm sure this information will be especially helpful.

For a free copy contact me at
1777 S. Harrison St., Ste. 625, Denver, CO 80210,
Phone #303-756-3599,
Fax #303-691-0474,
e-mail:RWDuffCLU@aol.com
web: www.mcomm.com/duff/.

Notes

RWD Enterprises Order Information

Money Magic With Annuities: Great Ideas for Creative Investors – a series of creative reader-friendly concepts for using annuities in financial planning. $19.95 + $6 shipping & Handling
Quantity Discounts Available for professionals wishing to share this book with clients. Please Contact RWD enterprises.

Other Publications by Richard W. Duff:

*Keep Every Last Dime: How To Avoid 201 Common Estate
    Planning Traps and Tax Disasters* (RWD Enterprises, 1998) + $6 s/h $ 36.95
Preserving Family Wealth Using Tax Magic: Strategies Worth Millions
    (Berkley, 1995) + $6 s/h $ 16.95
Taxes, Lawsuits and Family Conflict (Duff, 1994) + $7 s/h $ 89.95
*Great Ideas In Wealth Preservation: An Estate
    Planner's Manual* (RWD Enterprises, 1999) + $9 s/h $189.95
*The Annuity Blue Book: How to Avoid Hidden Traps & Tax
    Disasters When Selling Annuities* (RWD Enterprises, 1997) + $6 s/h $ 69.95
Annuity Reports:
    How To Use Annuities in Medicaid Planning $ 12.95
    *How Annuities Are Protected from Lawsuits and Creditors in the 50
        States* $ 9.95
    *A Taxing Situation: What Really Happens When An
        Annuitant or Policyowner Dies* $ 9.95
    Why Variable Annuities Are a Good Buy $ 9.95
    *Annuities and Insurance Values: Insurance Guaranty
        Fund Limits in the 50 States* (RWD Enterprises, 1999) $ 6.95
    Shipping and Handling on Annuity Reports: order up to $35 – s/h $6;
    $35.01 - $70 – s/h $12; $70.01 - $100 – s/h $20; $100.01 - $150 – s/h $30.
    Call for Shipping and Handling charges on Annuity Reports over $150.00.
                CO residents add 3% — Denver add 7.3%
                                                TOTAL_____

Name
_____

Address
_____

City, State, Zip
_____

Phone/Fax
_____

VISA/MC#   *Expires*
_____

Signature
_____

Or, make check payable to:
RWD Enterprises, 1777 S. Harrison St., #625, Denver, CO   80210
Phone (303) 756-3599 / Fax (303) 691-0474 / e-mail: RWDuffCLU@aol.com
Allow 2-4 Weeks for delivery

Richard W. Duff, J.D., CLU

Richard W. Duff, J.D., CLU, is a financial adviser in Denver, Colorado and is a principal in First Financial Resources (FFR). He is the author of *Preserving Family Wealth Using Tax Magic* (Berkley, 1995); *The Annuity Blue Book (How to Avoid Hidden Traps and Tax Disasters When Selling Annuities)*, 1997; and *Keep Every Last Dime, How to Avoid Common Estate Planning Traps and Tax Disasters*, 1998 (RWD Enterprises).

He can be reached at telephone 303-756-3599 or fax 303-691-0474.

RWD Enterprises Order Information

Money Magic With Annuities: Great Ideas for Creative Investors – a series of creative reader-friendly concepts for using annuities in financial planning. $19.95 + $6 shipping & Handling
Quantity Discounts Available for professionals wishing to share this book with clients. Please Contact RWD enterprises.

Other Publications by Richard W. Duff:

Keep Every Last Dime: How To Avoid 201 Common Estate
   Planning Traps and Tax Disasters (RWD Enterprises, 1998) + $6 s/h $ 36.95
Preserving Family Wealth Using Tax Magic: Strategies Worth Millions
   (Berkley, 1995) + $6 s/h $ 16.95
Taxes, Lawsuits and Family Conflict (Duff, 1994) + $7 s/h $ 89.95
Great Ideas In Wealth Preservation: An Estate
   Planner's Manual (RWD Enterprises, 1999) + $9 s/h $189.95
The Annuity Blue Book: How to Avoid Hidden Traps & Tax
   Disasters When Selling Annuities (RWD Enterprises, 1997) + $6 s/h $ 69.95
Annuity Reports:
   How To Use Annuities in Medicaid Planning $ 12.95
   How Annuities Are Protected from Lawsuits and Creditors in the 50
     States $ 9.95
   A Taxing Situation: What Really Happens When An
     Annuitant or Policyowner Dies $ 9.95
   Why Variable Annuities Are a Good Buy $ 9.95
   Annuities and Insurance Values: Insurance Guaranty
     Fund Limits in the 50 States (RWD Enterprises, 1999) $ 6.95
Shipping and Handling on Annuity Reports: order up to $35 – s/h $6; $35.01 - $70 – s/h $12; $70.01 - $100 – s/h $20; $100.01 - $150 – s/h $30. Call for Shipping and Handling charges on Annuity Reports over $150.00.
CO residents add 3% — Denver add 7.3%

TOTAL_____

Name
_____

Address
_____

City, State, Zip
_____

Phone/Fax
_____

VISA/MC#   *Expires*
_____

Signature
_____

Or, make check payable to:
RWD Enterprises, 1777 S. Harrison St., #625, Denver, CO   80210
Phone (303) 756-3599 / Fax (303) 691-0474 / e-mail: RWDuffCLU@aol.com
Allow 2-4 Weeks for delivery